HER MOON

A POETRY COLLECTION
HARPO MARTEL

ISBN: 979-8-9875535-7-2
FIRST PRINTING: FEBRUARY 2026

Micah Kielisch
COVER DESIGN

BROUGHT TO YOU BY
AW SHUCKS! PUBLISHING HOUSE

DEDICATED TO THE ONE WHO PULLS ME
DOWN TO EARTH AND LIGHTS MY ENTIRE SKY,
MY WIFE LEA NECOLE.

SUNDUST

My dearest Sundust
I beg you, never burn out
the moon already hides from me
but you shine your silt and silk skin my way
a billion specks to find you
in every nightfall

I hide so many things away while I wait for you
it has been such a long time

When I think the door is still locked
you hold the dark
beneath your cloak
assaulting the dude bros
in the back alley with the brightest light
your knight princess grip on my shoulders

I do not want
debris stuck in my eye
lint stuck in the iris
or wool lining on the lid
I can see

I do not want someone only
for their ability to perform
makeshift living room surgery
for this or
to remove a railing splinter
by the shine of a precision light

I do not want
a wiped 1985 floppy disk
of a temporary moon

I tell everyone
you may not still beam
the way you used to
but you do anyway

1251 MILES

This cityscape is a billboard advertisement
for my farfetched dreams
so I go
a feathered brush drags across
lengthy strokes of shadow work
east-west calling upons
are wild incantations of art
that no one thought could be made
outline the clouds
bend the light
teach the dark
to fly over your head
since you do not ever understand
that I am not over the moon
about this
I am not the cow to jump over it
I am not the man whose face is a circle
I am not someone who lands on the moon
I am not aware of the moon
I am not of the moon
I am never going to be interested in
getting up to praise
the fucking moon

STAND ME UP

The oak branch trembles
I'm freaking out again
a trend in all of my beginnings
this time because I have been alone four years
and cannot not stand another second

You add the kindling
and burn marshmallows for yourself
as you fume

My loneliness is always
too much of a production for you
and you make it known
through the way you move

Cancel for tonight
like you always do
pull the curtain and
quit

My desire for security
is pathetic
and the country club golf course
sees it in my eyes

Birds of Paradise out back
oranges and tap beer at church
a fat raise in your paycheck
gold star, you finally made it

STARRY NIGHT

The continuous concealment
is the easiest part
of stealing The Starry Night
in all black the smell of sweat lingers

keep the secret a secret
the dark helps you
you get away with it
for the next 6 birthdays

deep 'neath the bed where the frame rests
upstairs on the very corner of the Trail
though there is no real evil
you are a sinner for what you do

when the door closes you uncover
hang the precious painting on your wall
for the afternoon
chair under the knob
free to admire

you whisper
how sneaking is an art
you like the creativity and
the way it makes complex things look easy

a frown in a crown
we watch classic horror
only holding hands when someone dies

I am the pansy
beautiful because
it's a flower nonetheless

the sign on the door reads something unreadable
you deny the crime to the smear
top headline in the family newspaper
"Đisgraced Đaughter Cut from the Will"

The scents fill the air each Saturday
It is allowable today
for me to stay
eucalyptus mint
sweet potatoes on the grill

You tiptoe out after 3 am
til 5:22 light
escaping the sunlit corner of
the guest room
to the other side
where you praise the art
and give a critical conversation a chance

Wow! It's amazing!
Complement each other
compliment the color
of my eyes
in the absence of shame

STARRY NIGHT

it was there you insist the law is your bond
you throw the art back down
as the moon swims up

STARRY NIGHT

"THE SUN"

I could always pick you out of a lineup
a bright face in forced composure
I would squint to find you in a crowd
crawling along the turnpike at 5 AM
to try and catch you rising

one quick stroll in the middle of august
turns into a thousand miles
this makes the migraines almost unbearable

Somehow in those days eye damage looked cool
I mean the flare is so persuasive that
its charming me snake style
 a promise of
"Moon: Coming Soon"
flashes by
for a full nightcap of relief

My blindness to the disposition
was so dangerous
the sun became a quotation marksman

PATH OPERA

The path!
Oh, the agonizing and natural
ever turning path
long! And
far away

AWAY
from normal

I so dramatically say
THIS IS THE PLACE!
WHOA
Derangement
its core barely intact
zonk out
crash out
weird out
giving weird her full moment

Somehow she lights the way!

SPIN

I try to look over there
not too far off the edge
or I might go down too
and bonk my head real good
on another dirty bus stop shelter

Breaths of air from tiny stars
circle across the back of the Chevy
sights behind eyelids make galaxies
a wildly jealous lover
it's a vicious circle
I sit in my bucket seat drunk on spiced rum
I think of how to stop myself
I musn't tell the sister she's a bitch

Shit, it's still a party
I get there late
and sit by myself
while these white collar assholes
talk about the money in the room
I could get rich
in 4 months!
I hear advice on how to be a bigot
cocktail shrimp count

A lady sways in the back of the bar
Fifteen dollars for hypnotism... too dizzy to walk
ride the tilt-a-whirl of head cases
throw back the shots of tequila they can't take

EYES

A double spark, radioactive honeycomb
detonates something against my sense of humor
and stomps from claustrophobic edges of lashes
to the mammoth lily crashpads in mine

I run toward them like a child who hears the ice cream man
bells ring with wind chimes in sticky air

I stop so sudden when I reach the sound
I see them warp and go all the way to dark
then laugh as they outrun me
I've always been the fat kid with asthma

I let the tears salt my lips
they drip a rainfall of fire burn

I fall down then, and skin my knee
hot-concrete-joint marriage and divorce
meeting them again an 823rd time for only seconds

the tiny rocks and Already Been Chewed gum
that make up this path to Nirvana
tattoo my ankles red with their shards

and when I finally get the chance to look
3 blocks past my smashed, crooked glasses
I can no longer see them

I know that I am in love with them
so for the record
nothing burns or stings more
than to watch your spiral grooves
pull across the stylus
like ferns to the sun
turn away

EYES

BAD VIBRATIONS

Fallen and you can't get up
it's always tragedy after tragedy
your gym shorts on the couch
your loud ass mouth
your 17 dogs
they abandon you like everyone else has, huh?

She is perfect! Again
Has gravity
not caught up
to your tall-tale
life?

The Layton Avenue bitchfit
is always so expensive
but she gives up every time
the new supply runs out
Rolling over to be "alone"
on the ghost road
stealing your ex's car
putting it in drive
and shoving the money in the trunk
that belongs to everyone but you

the medication "saved you"
so you blow bubble gum
caricatures
on a Himalayan sea salt wedding day
to stay relevant

you can't get much closer
to being the disappearing jet smoke
special effects are still fake

everytime you fall
all your "friends"
fly like monkeys
and keep your ego lifted up

BAD VIBRATIONS

MOON SONG

Your brown eyes?
yes
love struck me
you loved me
like a meteor
like a surprise party
where I screamed
when I saw the animatronic pizza mouse
but won 1000 tickets
like a million dollars
that I'll never win
and never hold or see
but dollar bills stink anyway

Is this gravity?
yes
it's you
it's your little kid grip
it's your rosehips
shampoo
that pulls me in
like a star dipped in caramel
and wrapped in magnolias

When you smile?
yes
I can't function
I don't have any gum left
I won't walk the plank
I won't cartwheel off the edge
of the earth

This hold?
Magnetic pull
under
over
the bridge I grew up near
when they detonated
the section that broke
it was not louder
than my language
screaming
YOU ARE THE ONE

MOON SONG

TAMPA BAY

A hike in the city again
hands rest on my hips
sweat leaks into my eye
at the pier
with all this gear
and a canteen of pickle juice
for the cramps

JANSPORT
non ergonomic and
holds all my jokes
filled with all the
dumb voices
some multiple choices
and a rotten, shriveled banana peel
I am so god damn tired

I make a wish
to not be at the lake
or to not be away at all
walking in the heat alone
but here I am

she's at home

she's at home

Why now, so I wonder how thick the air is in Tampa?

I wonder what color her eyes are when the sushi reservation starts
I wonder how many times you lie to her to until the car door closes

Flat out, deliberate
We were supposed to go to Italy
I got my passport last year

I wondered how it felt to sleep in her bed
Now I wonder how she ever lived in my head

I still wonder if the dog was fed
I wonder if the dog is dead

TAMPA BAY

THE PINT

The tall window
at the coffeeshop that
started your obligation to me
is cracked today

I walk in half an hour
before closing and before
the interchange is clogged again

You push it all away and speed
back to the place
that is far enough away
where you think my words can't touch you

the song in the car knocks you back
right into the bathroom stall
where you throw back your Pint glass
and the lipstick stains my cheek

LIFE IS A DANCE

The to do list has got its hands on me
it pulls me down like
being picked last
and it always feels like
the free world and its contents
are too close in proximity

I feel like a squished bug go bye bye
a worker bee rogue
nothing but a victim of the 9-5
at a support group for burn out

The crowd is large here
must wear headphones and
forever pretend I am somewhere else

Too bored out of my gourd
to imagine anything different
or to wish for any space to stay
I promise that I
was up there once
higher than Mount Everest and
The Burj Khalifa

higher than the Hercules-Corona
Borealis Great Wall
when
I wrote it on my Smith-Corona
drinking our Corona

X

underwater on planet X
you needed luxury wheels for your birthday
exactly X years before
putting off the test
failing the test
and saying that was because of me

X marks the spot
solve it all here
do as I say
but get their car towed
to X your mind

you were finally getting somewhere
before you clawed your way back down
and pulled your own rug again
you gave up on me
and I X you for that
since no apology was given
if you even know what that is
if you even know who I am

but you do not
you do not know why I exist
just as X thought

you feel so tired like you said you would be
I thought I could trust your words
you feel so bored like you said you would never
but lo and behold! You do

I got fired
I feel so undesired
you can't hear me
because you are plugging your ears with X

the dreams you had last night
fall directly into your lap

I am never the anchor I try to be
I am a paperweight
you cut the ropes
and I float back down
to where you found me

you sell the story
to whoever listens
you drive your stake
deeper into the shoreline
and discard the X in the brush
pound the wounds into the sand
until
it all broke apart

NOW! Ultimately X equaled out to X
which does not mean a thing
at this point
but it put an end to it finally

X

I FEEL THE S(H)AME

I should not have flirted with La Florida
sipping and talking about how great
the jokes were there
on a caffeine binge
and they keep mansplaining
how laughter was medicine
but you stopped laughing
even when the punchline was funny
when the punch was too fruity for your Mom
when the punch was Mike Tyson voiced kung fu

I do not tell of my love for the Macabre
Astrology it's disguise
Ugh, people still think that means Astronomy
Whatever, Aquarian aloof

I do not tell people I love the chase
it can be faked as playing tag
I swear on my Grandma's grave
this isn't running away from responsibilities

I'm not just smart
I'm whimsy and hipster
The trip and fall on an orange peel?
Happens so quick,
before I even get a chance to grab a coffee

I'm like damn
was I ever really up there?

RAIN SOUNDS

The cat is rolling around
in the house I want
that looks just like
the one we slept on top of
the other night

The one where I sit
on the balcony just to be beside you with a book and a Breve'
until the sun sleeps by tossing and turning
and we might as well try to as well

Snapping back
Cause I'm sitting
at the edge of the bed
wiggling my feet to stay awake
waiting for you to climb back in
and sing songs
about weird things that you see in the room
so I don't start the looney tunes crazy
sob stories again
my medication's off and you know it

you pivot to stand up comedy
making up infomercials for bad wigs
and I laugh myself to tears
that wouldn't fit anywhere else
It's turn down service
it's turn on material
and the candle flickers behind your head
you hum indie songs and chug water

CAMPING

A backyard sticker burr on a spring a jacket
just kids tripping over the clothesline that fell again

A pancake
nailed to a tarp

No yo-yos and no dreams
with our runaway Lucky Charms
baggies of the shit
filled to the brim
and we hide behind the garage

tonight
we set up behind the bushes
with the cordless phone in the rain
we're scared again

the flashlight clicks to on
and we camp in the city
til it's quiet and we can sleep
in our own beds again

MIDNIGHT

Crooked dandelions splayed
out in a vase
actually a paper coffee cup
since that's all we have right now
they're wilted from being suddenly
plucked but you make them
look alive anyway
pouring Sprite in the bottom
and telling me who in your family
told you it works

You told me about Betty
and Bill squared
about the big pizza you used to share
before your dad passed away
how your Great Grandma got lost in the Smithsonian
and always looked like a celebrity

I told you about Margo and John
how they were in the air force
and the tale of their five daughters
who are all different in so many ways

The growth of the arabica
in your chest of treasures
makes your heart beat faster
and you go from this to that
always been tit for tat
but not with me

I GOT No LIGHTS
(TO HOLD ME DOWN)

The darkest nights have no stars
not even one to wish on
or catch a fall and pocket them

Pinocchio loses his noses
the bone exposes
stark white dig in the ground
paleontology

one touch by a moon chill that singes instead
there is no magic here, it is cold bitter nothing

fossil eyes
fossil lies
fossilized
"But it's okay!"
she says like someone who is a REAL GIRL
someone who is blessed
she explains away misunderstanding
she steals me away
"Two shadows can still meet
under the moon at noon in The Land
let's play! My weirdo! fate!"
till it's not anymore

Booby traps
line The Forest City
a gummy glue sticky-hand
smacks my neck to the wall

escapes with bell rigs
fake floor tiles and deadfall mechanisms
a malediction in an oil spill
scrawls across the staircase

the air is cool and the power's out

candles light up
guns load up
chant scream
scream chant
chant scream
as the house sleeps

table top tips
ghost gifts loom
the candles snuff out
I wake up

rhythmic devil taps on the door
he draws perfect pentagrams
on your good China

tell me again
how this shit isn't a curse

I GOT NO LIGHTS
(TO HOLD ME DOWN)

RIDE

Riding my bike from the South side
to the east side
I grab a cold drink
and guzzle it
like I hadn't drank in days
I gulp it like a frenzied fish
out of the water for now

Your words are sharp
they cut my head
into a jigsaw puzzle
clipping coupons inside
nature's discounted thoughts

this was really hard to put together
it took hours and hours
to find the pieces
because they were hidden all around
it took glue
the school kind that I'd
peel n stick on my hands
making a life mosaic
that turned to garage trash
after it was done
it took everything in me
not to go back to the table

I unlock my bike from the frozen bars
I ride home cold and clammy
not thinking of you again until now

PAD THAI

I was never sure how to make Pad Thai

You made the sandwiches
and threw them in the trash
Milwaukee Michael Jordan
when I was on my way home
because they weren't hot

You think limes are horrendous
but you bought them
you cut them
you squeezed them
and you took off your clothes

I have never had rare steak before
and if I had
I never took a bite
long enough to actually taste

We signed the walls of the kitchen
and the dining room
to see the paint again, next time we go

DARK BLACK

Submersed, bitch.

Completely swept up
into the mess

relatable honestly
Which color covers you up
and tucketh you in?

Not just black

dark black

gorilla primer
coal miner

obsidian soot
raven midnight
pitch
vantablack

nightmares
If I wear the tux to mourn your virtue

gray hairs
if I try to please you

at this point I am the void
I avoid you like Jehovah at the door

You are a void check
that people try ro cash
at the 7 ELEVEN

But not me
I am drenched, darling in this peace
and serving
"I care not"

DARK BLACK

Violet Heart

the long day falls
into the arms of the night
of those who know not what to expect
a mix of red and blue
the night sky hue
the family, nails down to the quick
huddle in a clump
no one says a word

a heart shaped mylar shines in the corner
sticky to the broken ceiling
the sliding moon door brings a breeze
lub dub
in the corner hospital room
its only light the carss zooming past
every couple hours

get well soon
spelled out by cut up paper
that is barely seen without reading glasses
I purchased them an hour ago
and did not save the receipt
instead I crumple it into a ball
my sadness plays hackysack in my mind

a getaway car waits outside
it looks like a good escape
it might take you
to heaven

fully equipped with sitcom reruns
and the saltiest potato chips
resting at the bottom of the bag
waiting to be crushed

or maybe to hell
where you must clean your teeth after every meal
and run generic errands
the following Sunday morning
cry and sweat after simply getting dressed

the chance to live is wrapped in expensive paper
like a shiny gift everyone should want
to open
ribbon unravels to reveal
collateral damage and
something your sister had delivered

it draws new veins
where it burned its enemies
and no one wanted it to go
trickle trickle
inside and out
continues to pump violet

VIOLET HEART

MOON JUICE

These wiry wisps of hair
a spirit waning from the swamp
fall into my face
whiplash
strandstand
I'm a book
 you ban from existing

alley-oop and dunk you win
roundest moon in the basket
I pretend this is an all out vibe
In perfect historical accuracy
she talks about her art
like she's the next big thing
she's a Claude Monet
she's a crystal cut into the shape of a fox

she sits on her perch, proclaiming to all
that I look like I believe it

Take her for every word
eyes glaze over
some kind of mountain she climbs
she oozes delusions and drinks from my cup
she gulps it down like
koolaid on a summer night in 99
great bluedini
purplesaurus rex
refreshing
Jonestown or something

The color of the cup,
is light and opaque
you totally
get the vibe of my tattoos
but you loathe who I am
at my core
You sip me through a straw
so you don't have to taste my bandaid soup

I pretend to like this
I light myself on fire
I bury the good times
in the neighbors backyard

Chinese fire drill
Stop drop roll
get down on the ground
stray bullets

The charm is a series
of unfortunate events and
I swear I see a comet fly past two times
I cannot catch them on camera
you say they are snitches
and they go to a hospital for stitches
I clean it up

explosion
explosion
Let go of my hands
I am chewing tobacco and gum
spit rat, tit for tat

MOON JUICE

SLEEPOVER

A game played on burlap
you sit in my lap
just long enough before
the sun fully sets
my feet fall asleep
pins and needles stab
each of us jab
at the other
in the place you first read my cards

I'm not a size 2 and not even a size 12
but you don't care
you tell me that my body is but a vessel
for what lies inside

My flaws are out in the open now
and I don't really know what to think
I pretend to be uninterested
play my Tamagotchi, drag my pen
while you're trying to tell me a story
all so I don't need to make eye contact
and you might just give up

It's already 6 AM and no one
is thinking of sleeping
because what if we miss the Paleta man?
What if I wake up
and the neighborhood cat has been at the window for hours
begging for something to eat?

LUNAR LOUNGE GALA

A moonrock sits on the corner
of my shelf not once asking me
why I said that thing in 2014
we've been best friends since Tuesday
a simple understanding between matter
and a soul
It hasn't raised an eyebrow
It hasn't raised kids
It hasn't raised a glass, to me

What if people were
heavy on presence
and lighter on opinions
but not like the olden days
not like when kids were to be seen
not heard

I host dinner parties
where no one talks softly in the kitchen
we mime our hot tea
like we're in the Parisian streets

I serve silence in the duck blood soup
no one asks if it's gluten free.
we sip our lunar tea in beakers,
masking that its La Croiix
because lunar drinks sound mysterious
but La Croix is fancy and sober

Poets set up clackety old machines
in the middle of the plaza
where no one is in a rush
I'm talking a few billion years to spare
they write answers to
what's on your mind?
and they have not a bother
because they are rocks

and that's why you trust them
I give everyone a name
something fancy
we write poems
like Rocks are Fancy Dirt
and The Origin of Birds
Let's read them in The Lunar Lounge
while the dinosaurs
find out they become chickens
and roll over in their graves near the party

LUNAR LOUNGE GALA

CAUTION:HOT

The supreme cup of warmth
a golden brew for the days
stained to my lips
espresso

In the middle of my panic attack
I can't speak and my brain says "somethings missing"

The train departs
it zooms past to get over that other way
to get to where it's best I don't

I wait ouside as you rummage through the bags again
for something to pacify the baby

I down more caffeine
or something

I worship the ground
you tiptoe on
and I gulp
it burns

You stomp two feet down with all your might
all over the frog in my throat
ribbit ribbit
squish squash
pish posh

ABDUCT ME

Let me call you baby
til the aliens come back

Let me wrap my arms around you
til I superglue to your bones

Hands scream fusion
Space screams illusion

THIS SIDE UP

My hair was finger length
when you turned
my heart
on its head

It's the first headstand
like a whistle
like a snap
like a knot
tightly spun
The vibrations sprawled
like branches
reaching
blood comes
rushing
body upside down

Routes dissolving
lifting directions off
of skin

The ship tips sideways
and flips
like a coin

The comedown would prove magnificent
from a height that is significant
reaching over the top
long enough to fly me up
to the other side of this

FLOWERMOON

Lilacs and cherries on street signs
Tree sap and weeds
newly grown branches wink down from above
blanketed green, and blue

sweet smells wander
stems come alive like dancing auroras
sharp as mint and scissors
cool on the eyes, and blurry
for they only come out at night

here come those nocturnal sparrows too
the night blooming with vines
goodbye bi-polar-bear weather
a gift horse exists
but bites craters in your finger, and laughs

each blade of grass and each blade of crass
tells a story of displaced bugs
ladybugs lay atop
then creeps in that feeling, of crime
like when we thought he placed the flag

carrying plants from one side to the other
 sleep has been replaced
awareness goes undercover, under the flowerbed of thoughts

FANCY SHIT

I say that it's just business
then watch their eyes go glassy

I pocket bills and jewelry
I smoke cigars
a gal with a chain necklace
keep this shit classy

Don't ever change
cause heavens a joke
and people are fake

I reach into your bag
Searching for bread
an heirloom ring
you think I'm charming
you think I'm clever

I chew on your trust
I bite your heart
right off your sleeve

I leave teeth marks
for everyone to see

TIE ME DOWN

the universe holds so much inside
but you do not try to look beyond
your reflection
it's a woe man all the same

come on and give it a whirl
whirlybirds laugh from above
hold your breath until purple pines emerge
brain bursts out
hits every branch
on the way down
just like when you fall again
from the evil tree
and I run down like syrup
slow
slow
slow

Switch off the volume
with your foot
each toe
in it its own sock hole

Congratulations in order for
getting me
right where you want me

1. Subdued
2. Quiet
3.Blind

POCKETS

I wear a Beethoven nametag
"Hello, my name is"
but at least I got famous
by not talking and not seeing

I did not come here for nothing
but you fix that mighty fast
minnow speed dating
and bitching and moaning

I get a lot more than what is in your pocket
dryer lint from the trap
cursed stones
tiny religious texts
a precious coin
slimy ass snake skin
magic beans cause this means jack shit to you

dramatic savior flair
dramatic victim flair
pick the shiniest wax apple

WHERE THE HELL WE ARE

You do not know me from Eve
my sharp edges turned velvet knives
you let me stay

The day I met you
the moon fills the morning
and the coffee cools

there is no more time
to drink it down

it's decaf but you make it feel the same

you ponder the future
and make us a meal

When I walked in that night
I got on my soapbox and said
"You came all this way
after always pulling out the roots
to anchor them down right here."

You light up like NYC
you give me a key

6 months prior
I wait lovesick in a parking lot
I was so far from a plan
I was so far from you

A charming rebel
travels for what feels like forever
with a wish to touch a single flower
to keep it from wilting

The sun finally shows its face again
as it always does with time

WHERE THE HELL WE ARE

AUTOMATICA

The forest drinks its forest drink
listening to the language
of moths and mirrors
tracking and relaxing on whispering time
Sediment covered in blankets
where round mementos lie down

if ever there is sunlight
maybe the trees can bow in unison
silver beams trace outlines in the rock
for essays yet to be written

a crumpled leaf blows on its own
but not before passing its shapeshifting cousin
how many of these are there?

Will the world hide the amount?
will the life forms destroy them?
will the animals be jealous?
there are no yes or no answers

there is a creek, ushing and cool
steam billows up when the air is hot
the breathwork of the earth
slowly syncing to the beat of life

the origin will speak
well, the origin will fly
and the bones and the fragments
and the crisp pages follow

THE DEVIL WILL PULL YOU DOWN TO HELL BY YOUR HAIR

The science never ends
it moves across the sky
is the earth flat?

Is there a single nerve ending of our own
that would even trust the answer from you?
You leave us left to figure it out on our own
like everything else you are
supposed to teach

Maybe you should go
look it up in the encyclopedia
while I entertain the vacuum salesman at the door
I am too depressed
I am too stressed
and maybe you should stop
spraying so much perfume
and maybe you should stop
singing at the dinner table
because he will pull you down

Or maybe, you should be more like
your sister
Or maybe, you should do the things
I like to do
or don't
so I can ignore you more

Is there a benefit of you
if it's no benefit to me?

LIVING UP HERE

Existentialism
Kombucha addiction
Misanthropia

Fine

GOODBYE

233 DEGREES CELSIUS

a malleable figure
that does not love the kiln

heat means hardness
permanently

Stay upright
the requests seem uptight

give ultimate wonder
with no on switch

seven whole weeks
only one touch

it is said that
grateful hearts always win

only, the truth is
warmth is required

or figures can freeze
shadowed craters for good

BLACK HOLE

The most perfect prize stares into the bathroom mirror
shiny shine wannabe gold
perspiring onions peel back only slightly

abstract
or is it not giving a fuck?
parallel lines break
draw them in code like they mean something
Damn, it's not Shakespeare!

trace it all
with your own glitter glue from childhood
sculpture of a brain, blessed only by confidence
imagination cannot manufacture itself
lick up those spicy bites of dust
feel the envy simmer
darkness is not depth
it is a black hole
arrogance plays hide-and-hide

JOKES ON YOU

When I found out you could kill centipedes
I wanted to put your picture in the dictionary
Soulmate: The one who kills centipedes 4 U

You hate Rachel from upstairs
you're sick of her shit
like the landlord cares, so
you saw your way out through the bathroom ceiling
like she needs her floor

my cheekbones fall out
when you twerk to TV theme songs
and when I tell you stories
so do yours
our smiles morning light
late at night

You lost your vape in the couch again
and it's too far of a walk to grab another
there's been a sudden snow squall, so
you make Chicken and Dumplings until summer

I'm not supposed to eat gluten
and come to find out neither are you
so we take turns taking care of each other
Death Row by gluten
RIP to our cuddle puddle
and our bathroom

STORM SONG

I gave you flowers on Rose Lane and
tried to love you on Appaloosa
You poured out the lava
and I jumped
to catch ash after ash
with my bare hands

The fire burned all of the bushes that night
you still complained about the cold
rotating just as you said you would
if my perfection unraveled
and pulled away from the bone

Stupidly, I cried,
"She was a part of the sky, wasn't she?"

Well here she comes

Tornado in town
chasing it down
picking me up and throwing me for
a loop

COMMANDER

My midnight June
mixtape lover face
My time napper
flying past-er
when it's a good time

Hand against my heart
cross it at the
Taco truck cocktail party
in the arts hotel lobby
where we stargaze on the rooftop

Wherever you came from
before you were here at the lake
Take me to your leader or
become one to me on this eve

KALEIDOSCOPE

The wrong side of the telescope
things appear further than they actually are

tripod rests at the top of the top
toward 95% water
and the watermelon patch
over on highway F

Waves obscure fully
and full the Earth's mouth with water
to satisfy her thirst once more

Crop circles swallow seagulls whole
Coral disappears under blankets of her fog

Stop signs warn of no stops
River lines innocently lie
it the longest blue
turned to orange, turned to maroon

Pyramids point the finger toward heaven
Chocolate Sno-cap mountaintop crunch

all the cities at night
grids of fireflies

COUNTING SHEEP

Ɖarts fly
at a Christmas tree
and land in the trash that
lays on the floor of the sleep lab
where little hands try
to muddle through the mud pies
and beat the insomnia out of me
maybe it will
get better

clouds above the bed
maybe a light rain
Nope
a free fall
because do not hit the ground
in a dream

Apply the 14k gold peel mask
the hair treatments
those stupid little eyelash curlers
and watch videos full volume
to keep me awake

I've been caught
6 soda pops in my hand
at the gas station off Fulton Ave

the police come to mark down words
phone rings 45 more times
 I cannot answer

Bottle cap torque
wings and pitchfork
picket sign and blow torch
hint water on the porch

Not the one in the way one would think
Halo
twisted up into
a circle of hell energy
so divine
its all I need to shine

Make things up
Before and after
Selfish and a liar
A moving force, a physics fail
A loyal pet, dead and off the grid
A broken spirit, a free thinker
A breaker of bird wings but I command it to fly
Saturday morning in the 216, night in the 414
Having no fun, having the time of my life with a wife
Cleaning up blood, Cooking salmon stir fry
Gathering knowledge, an abuser accuser
Believing it all for nothing, lying for safety
I am going nowhere, I am everywhere
with a stopwatch and a smile
I fall asleep

COUNTING SHEEP

BIG FINE

Tickets to ride
no one knows the cost
I give my very last dollar bill
to take you up and
take you out
just to twirl you around twice

coins in the machine
cards on the table
lights and sounds
humidity soaks my hat
I gamble on this forever

You handle it at first
like a champ
the sparkling dresses
and glasses of wine
we're lost again

I pay the ticket
I pay the fine

I give up all my winnings
from that night
so you can have it all

SALTED EARTH

crashing
against the rocks

the waves of you

wash over her face
and burn her eyes

Heaven's Lake

Sunken into quicksand
teeth to a peach
delicate and peaceful
unserious but alluring

Cosmic crisp trees
make patterns
of light
sun soaked skin
 Vitamin U

Feelings develop slow
like photographs
juicy fruit
lipstick prints
concessions and confessions
iced coffee kisses

SMALL

I look
with a monocle
with binoculars
a monocular
that I remember as a telescope
I am bionic

The division starts a zigzag
it's more like a sidewalk crack
now I have no backbone

I am still
trying to figure out
how to get my laundry detergent into the car
without it spilling everywhere
and crying in the driver's seat
listening to meditation music
on the way home

This world is bigger than me
it has proved way too fucking big
I can't ever turn off the GPS
What was a degenerate do before this thing?
Get a grip Tom Tom

At least I have
a seven dollar 16 ounce sugar free vanilla latte on the way

CRAVINGS

The clock strikes nine
it's Sunday
and it's hard to finish your list alone
cooking and cleaning
Facetiming you at the grocery store
writing me into your narrative

The others turned toward you
flowers desperate for a drink
praise and money
sprayed your lies with honey
and I could only show my face
when I dissolved

Even then I could only show half of me
call me Two Face
I'm a double agent
the smaller half (a section)
a different fraction completely
who gets left in a box overnight
I guess if you like cold pizza that would be fine
Stale, hardened crust that breaks your teeth
just enough to keep around when you get hungry

SANDFIRE

Some do not like sand on the blanket
but like being on a blanket
in the sand

Some do not like more than 4 people
in this world
but can ignore the other 3
when given the world

Some do not like the bottom of the lake
and all it holds
but they like that familiar feeling of squishy toes
finding the bottom of the lake

Some do not like when the fire burns out
and all the smoke
and the mess
but they like the burn of the fire
while it goes

PREDICTABLE SCRIPT

Freckles fly and other speckles try, in reverse
braids of sage and crushed lavender plants
litter the ground from here to there
and someone picks them up not knowing
their vibrations lost balance and trip the cord
I want to tell them it's useless to trust you
but instead they follow you

Armies of leaves and branches bow
to a gas lamp like yourself
quickly covered by proof
 you lived a little
you eat cold miso soup
the doorbell records you both coming in
you forgot your keys were
glow-in-the dark
you forgot tonight I was insecurely attached
to the security system and you

Handcastles

Hands are all the trend
but can we make the next one
 a home in a person?

Can we take your moats and your oaths
and give them other names
for what you bring to the table?

Can we take "I love you" and pump it full of energy
full of sand from The Great Lakes
so that every time I pass you those words
we hold it down

Hands got nothing on what we have built
but they're everything on me, all the time
and when they craft their home
they unravel
every bit of thread from this frayed fabric

pick me up and carry
all my pieces like treasures
set gently on the pedestal
used to display angels

IMPRESSION

Sediments dust fingerprints
unearthed native patterns mark a time
they should grow up in too

A favorite color
might be brown

No atmospheres
No tectonic drift
No life lived

Impressionist embedding
stiff bodies and stems
reach and grab for hands
succumb
impossible to look at
yet somehow so familiar

Why can't I breathe?

residue clings
to the ends of the ones
we forget to give life to
but survive exile all this time

RIVER SONG

You held my hand
as the boats went by

I knew the city was the moon
when it lit up the wish you had
since you were seven

Role call tonight
your name came up last
and told you to watch

At the water
you peer closely on the pier
while I smile and nod
to the current herself

The silence said what it needed to

The river was the main attraction
and our attraction
turned out to be
a shiny distraction
of satisfaction
that night

I listen
and I fall in
I listen to you sing Leon
and I wanna go

She broke your gaze
from the sweeping
and you turned toward the bottom

Cupping hands to say
"This was the best night I ever had'
you'd love to see her again

Letting go of my hand briefly
your shoes came off
I didn't see you for minutes then
you hung up the phone

The city was your home

STREET OF THE SKY

It's 12:19 PM and you already don't want to be here

Your fresh panda shoes and your lined facial hair
you feel okay in the mirror

At 12:23 you get on your bike
pedals, sweat, swear words and no hope

the sky looked green while the ground looked blue
 a blank slate

My scream scares you more than the rolling impact
you said you were fine and your spokes were intact

You hug me and you did not know me
I shook, and you told me you had been through worse

I try to learn your name
I try to beg you to stay

You try to lose
but I do not win
you disappear into the alley
I lose my North

VANDAL

The tree leaks sap
and you make sure it's gone
because you are thirsty
and quite insane
you are a combination lock

You trample the leaves
that lay so sweetly on the ground
You do not notice the crunch

They press themselves down to force entry
to the start of the unknown
up is down
tagging names in the dirt
drinking spray paint
colorful crazy
high and hazy
disintegration
vandalism

DIAMOND

Sing a song of dreamlike state at the inception reception
LA ĐI ĐA LA LA
break her out of there
She's gonna be on Broadway, baby

Oh no
She's not
OVER MY ĐEAĐ BOĐY
They'll eat her alive

That took her head outta the clouds

She settled solid into a rock
and in her plan
they'll eat her dead

A ten on the Mohs
so you cannot crack her
like crème brulee
with a silver spoon

she can sing her songs of peace at breakfast

FAULT LINES

A high pile of dust and rocks
domino down
and make the same noise
my brain does
when it tries to make sense
of everything I hear
about guilt

Even in perfect stacks
stones fall on
physics
logic
a whim

entire architecture
toppled

I DIG YOU

I did not expect to find you
down in the dirt
where earthworms have their homes
crawling into small sleeping holes
to make hiding places for their crumbs

it's proved better than gold to dig
midswirl of the tree trunk
honey, smoke, and rust

smells fade down
into the layers
two treasures underground
buried in the very same place
for me to find and flood

SECRET BEACH

The bluffs look like mountains
which I was told
don't exist in Wisconsin
but apparently they do

The sun sinks into bed
behind the rock's shoulders
their love affair exposed in July

Evergreens, fish, and driftwood
bones and art yet to be found
we search for hours
sand sticks to our ankles

The gravel runs thin
like patience
and excuses

Money
flying out the window
as we drive down the road
to our hidden picture perfect shore

KARMA CAFE

A streetlight pole with bugs inside, their goopy glass veranda
I sit underneath when I tell you exactly how I need you
to like me

You play guitar, I smoke my cigars
that you tell me are cigarillos, you know it all

You sing to me in my secret place
and when the door slams
I ask you if you'll stay
I didn't really mean it but
you took that to heart

You uncork the wine
with a butter knife
and we laugh about our friends
and the way they de string their celery
on Wednesday nights
You keep saying I treat you like
a book without a title
but that's fine
I did not ask you to live on my shelf

For a time
I feel like the coolest kid
I get black ink
and dress up to impress

I do it all with words
and your favorite Italian dish

BECOMING

When becoming a rock
you don't get to decide anything
you can't move or speak
you must stay stone
statue, shoulders bowed

The change is slow, erosion
still, transformation
and now you exist for others

A hazard, to trip on
A project, to flip on

When becoming a rock
you must be solid
present
you must handle being ignored
but also ignore impact
you must take the hits with no visible marks

you must not help shape the landscape
but you must be warm to the touch
but you must be cold to your bones
impossible

you must be denied every and any drop of humanity

REUNION

Here's me again panicking
beetles infiltrate the party
beetles
even though they have names
and families
and feelings

They were never taught to stay away
from strangers
like I was
or railroad tracks
or places people were eating

Moss grows under the table
they shoo it all away
they sit among wildflowers
and demand to belong

CRUEL SUN

I search my catalog
for a poem about the water

Fingerprints stick
to the door of a place that
we met up a few times
after we traded back keys
on Brady Street

Coffee without milk
 a night with no curfew
 it's hot bitterness melts
all of the ice into summer

We ran down the stairs
and there were not enough dollars
to make the change needed
but at this point
their two cents did not matters
when they saw us waving

Sunglasses folded with their arms crossed
worn in the daylight and
hitting the cracked parking slab and burning
a short distance from your Nissan

I call you at bar time
You leave at breakfast
I buy two iced coffees and you try to find a motive

BOOTH STREET

We walk up the road
the opposite way of the one-way
rebels against the winds

Your dainty little necklace
holds the energy it took from me
when I explained myself to you

ATTENTION

You cannot bring yourself
to throw anything away

I can't bring myself
to stop talking or
finish a task
unless it's urgent

You don't wait
a second longer than the sun
takes to set
to say "Stop It"
and marry an aspiring minimalist
who can't remember
when her appointments are

I want your attention like gravity shows the moon
 pull me to you without question
I focus on you
and you keep me too

MIXED DRINKS

I can't stand the cat
but I'm willing to try
I even buy her stuff
like she's a new obsession
5 years later
she's my best friend
each morning I give her water

Rewinding
I'm feeling trapped fast
I'm pouring the signals of mixology in your mug

I like you
I don't know

I've never had anyone cook for me like this
I insist on going out for dinner alone

Let's move in
I can't fit my desk in here

Let's hang out
I'm terrified to be close to anyone

I bring you shish-ka-bobs
I don't want anything serious

You're my soulmate
I run back home by ten

SURRENDER

I don't hate the cat anymore
Now I hate myself
for ever thinking
I needed to get away from this
it was never a cage
it's my bedroom

So unorganized
the side of your bed where I sleep
is littered with papers
there's screws in my jeans
when you do the landry
we're still not sure where they ever came from

My life is a mess like for real
I lost my keys again
I forgot my work badge
I don't know where my water bottle went to
Somehow though you always do

I sit down with the candles burning
and write down ideas for us
We plan dates
I bring bruschetta and you bring Topo Chico
the lime and the bubbles are everything together

I hate picnics because
I hate bugs even more
when bees show their yellow jackets
you best believe I'm already down the block

CALL IT A SONG

Her hands smell of red clay
Her mouth tastes of black honey

I kiss the horizon
and fall deep all autumn long

The rhythm was off but it was a song

MOONWALKERS

I tell you that I loved another woman
on the church stairs

There are 32 of them
and with each step I count how many times
I wish for the courage to tell you

When it finally comes out
you do not
look at me like I am attracted to you
and you are not lemon, bro
you laugh and you tell me
that you smoked weed every night

We joke
and we toke
and we wear dresses
to stand up up up
in each others weddings

I beg and make you pinky swear
that next time you do this
I can be myself
and still stand on your side
jn my space suit

Home

Considering the weather here this morning
the lake sure does make
the city
look pretty
and feel less like
somewhere I need to escape

I always wish something was different here
the sky was a little wider
the sun a little kinder

But when it sparkles like it sparkles
and says what it says
speaking in that Caribbean blue
steel drums on my mind

I am a fish
a water bug
a ripple chasing herself

I'm five

Ten more minutes
the sun hasn't set yet, Mom
I made friends
the tide is low
big tall grains
a wave show
At Thirty-five
I live and love here

MAGNETIC

Why do you poke your mouth out
Have you gone mad?
I am feeling mad cool at least
Setting the table to have a tea party
Gummy worms and pop culture trivia
You need space? Call up Jupiter.
Then just like that no one says a word

Irish Coffee and spiked tea
neither of us drink
but we still act drunk
so please spill all of the secrets of why
you feel like you can't come to me
you name your demon
so that I don't think it's you
and so you don't think it's me
stupid plaques with stupid words
we aren't farmhouse aesthetic
we are magnetic

you grew up in the sticks
but you're more classy than me
No kidding
Merlot to my cheese

I grew up on a nice block
but I might be a loser
Nah, that's what the world tries to make you believe
I believe in ridiculousness
I believe in a loud mouth at the right place at the right time
mostly I believe in giving up

HA! I mean, on things that no longer serve me anymore
which is something we both agree on
I know that's a relief for us both
we are never 10,000 miles apart in our queen bed
its the perfect size
No Kings in this lair
the cooking shoes must go on

There's no point in ever questioning
definition of perfection in our hand written dictionary
we are the imperfect perfection
positive and negative attraction
there is no one else I would rather stare at silently
until we set the pride to the side and align and hug

MAGNETIC

BRAINS

Everyone always says
you've got me
in the palm of your hand
but I think you've got me
wrapped around your brain
it's just so weird like mine
you are 2000s fine
with your tramp stamp tattoo
and my eyebrow piercing
whew, we are those people

You make me feel like a million bucks!
Oh boy! Have I won on a scratch off?
Now we could fix the creaky floors
in this first level apartment
which could quite possibly
make us appear normal
well we need the landlord's permission
so nevermind
I will just waterboard myself
and you'll rip your skin off
back room lobotomies
studying our psychology
striving for oikonomy
free shitty economy
three years married
three years carried
three years buried
trichotomy

CORPORATE WORLD PEACE

I am me and not going anywhere
I can't meet the mark but

Every morning I wake
and make memories that will last
the rest of my life
sat a computer typing the same things over and over
ravishing

I brush my teeth at 7:42
because I must start work at my basement desk at 8:00
I meditate for peace at 7:27 because of the day I had yesterday

I rise from my corpse pose
I become a one eyed pirate zombie bitch
at 6:59 because I always seem to
come alive one minute before the alarm clock does

There's no dopamine in the mornings
sun's barely out in Milwaukee
nothing but gray
Jesus Christ I'm gay
three months out of the year
no
always
I meant three months of gray
in Milwaukee

Dr. Doctor
can you give me something
that will help me sleep?

He just tells me to make that money
get the hell out of here
do something greater
or you won't be shit

PROMISES

You like to tell ME
all of the things I've been through
but what you don't know
is that I didn't have a cent to my name in 2018

I certainly had fake promises
a journal full of dumb shit
parking tickets up the wazoo
a lot of potato chips and friends

an obsession with astronomy
a wish for some autonomy

now you know

MILLENNIAL BLUES

Hang in there chump
we can stare at people in public
anytime you want
we can sit in her living room
saying nothing
that's what my best friend says
but she's hundreds of miles away

Why is it so hard
to make good friends in your 30s?
when you don't drink cherry bombs
or spend all your doll hairs to own a boat

People only want me
like they're making a Pop Tart
Instant Gratification
they get hungry an hour later
once their sugar comes back down

People only want me
like they want the song to just CHANGE ALREADY

I am dull and boring
and apparently do not evoke
enough thrill to sustain them

OOPSIES

I many not remember
feeling this embarrassed in 20 years
but its sitting in my living room right now
and it pays none of my bills
it just relaxes, stoic
unforgiving
with it's hat pulled down over its eyes
holding on to the couch I got on the internet
it can't let it go if it tried

Somehow this is shocking to you
and everyone else too
but it's all I've ever known

Different dreams taking seats
taking drags
at my "vintage" dinette table
I reach for the tiny candies
resting in the helmet
they fall into the ashtray and rot

The conversation doesn't leave the room
the red cheeks really broke the ice
kind of like
what happens in this house stays in this house
I stay ashamed and unarmed
all by myself

ANXIOUS ORIGINS

Back in the day
when people breathed through iron lungs
makeshift respirators were experiments
and no one was thinking of me

The inventors were born
like the babies were
their moms fell asleep by chloroform
their pain taken by opium

they tried to find a cure for diseases
tool shed full of ice picks and saws
creating genetic brain failures
that would one day mutate
and manifest themselves
as the type of anxiety
first found in me
I too started from science
the hesitant bang

I'm famous
take my autograph
I can use my metallic marker
to make it more worthless than beanie babies
and my stamp collection
I can lick it and slap it on
the back of you like a sign
that says
"KICK ME"

THE BREAKWATER

At half past one
will you meet me at the lake?
There's needles on the shore
probably algae too
You REALLY don't want to swim in there
I say
but you're already knee deep
in 50 degree water
and splashing yourself in the face

It's June and
the sun will surely burn your cheeks
you'll warm you up
we can sit and talk
on the bench right here
about things
you haven't told anyone else in Milwaukee

I'm running out of time
I shuffle around to find my keys
to leave
I drop my phone
and cracked the screen
this is the real me

I left my car windows open and it rained
so I stayed to watch the stars

Heaven forbid I'll be late for
the last few minutes of virtual tic-tac-toe
at the virtual company party
surrounded by people who have
virtually no personality
Virtual Ghosts Inc.

I live 4 minutes away
bicycling it takes 40

I always do this
you just don't know that yet

You have not run out of questions
I shout and scream the answers
as I pedal away
You're confused and you stay

THE BREAKWATER

CUPID'S ARROW

I have seen the orchard crying
right after it storms
sopping wet
mopping up the pond water
branches hanging and torn
like a limb off my dad
when he's sad
he'd pay an arm and a leg
for me to never cry
he would never sell me off like that
to marry a dude
cause he has always accepted me
for who I am
bad apple or not

the leaves shine when its humid
the fruit splits open
spilling juice into the dirt
when it hits
face water on my shirt
I'm very hurt

the lightning struck my dog
you told me slurring, in a fog
she'll miss me
and so will you

You took the keys and all the dishes
you kept the memory box
really didn't give a shit
about respecting my wishes

You tell me that I'm always welcome
You pull back the bow

Well screw that
I won't be coming back
so you can use my hands again

This was an inside job
Mafia ties
I am not being facetious
or fictitious
though I wish that I was
paper chains were the only motive

CUPID'S STUPID ARROW

GOODNIGHT

Crinkly
Crackly
Fire in the hole
so it's where I throw
my own death party
I left directions in my
nightstand drawer
for me to find
when my attention deficit
was chilled out for the night

I have the service
at the lake
where I drank fortified wine
for the first time as a minor

Where my car got stuck
in the Winter of 2020
on the night of the full moon
when I drove too close to the ice to see it rising
my brother showed up
shovel in hand to dig me out
and he said "bitch, you're dumb"

I got married in the same exact place as that
and it was lucky that my wife
was okay with that
all of my biggest memories are now in that park
even the ones I hate

Here lies this person
who thinks her infatuation with this park is special
an inappropriate funeral for my old self
so I'm not dead

there's show tunes playing
my siblings do the Charleston
til one kills the other

my nieces laugh at their own jokes
this is not their idea of plans with me
I wink in their direction and they're crying

They find my old journal
they love the new me
they wipe their eyes and they go to college
and they'll feed me sushi when I'm 85

That journal wraps its spiral around and around and
around
snakebites
small plates for all
hot chips and Mountain Dew
so unrefreshing but it's my favorite on Shark Week when
I'm 16

I'm reborn
I eat ribeye steaks
I ride my bike
I stay home
I howl at the moon
and I have 3 good friends
who like me for my money
or to say goodnight   GOODNIGHT